My Uncle Nathan

Wit and Wisdom

Written and illustrated by

Jerry McKee Bullock

DEDICATION

This book is dedicated to our children:
Ronnie, Randy, Roddy, Kathy, Kevin,
Kelly, and Kristie

And to our grandchildren: Amanda,
Brandie, Christopher, Christian, Darien,
Diana, Heather, Jordan, Kylie, Lydia,
Lindsay, Meredith, Natalie, Nathan,
Nicholas, Sarah, Shannon, and Zachary

Most importantly, this book would not exist without the
encouragement and the hours of hard work of Lucille, my wife and
the mother of our seven children. For 68 years she has stood by my
side and has been a part of every significant event of my life. This
little book took many hours of her time. She typed the manuscript
several times. She read it and reread it to ensure its grammatical
perfection. I depend on her to keep my thoughts clear and readable;
she does that to perfection. Besides that, she is the love of my life.

CONTENTS

FOREWARD

My father's family came to Texas from Louisiana in a covered wagon in 1867. They settled in the Steep Hollow community near the city of Bryan in Brazos County. Three of the sons left Brazos County. Joseph, the first one, and his family went to Lampasas and remained there. My grandfather, John C.B. Bullock, was second. In about 1887 he embarked on a seven-year trip to Scurry County. That is another story.

Nathan, our hero in this book, was last. He was ordained to the Gospel ministry in 1894 and followed his call to the west.

Uncle Nathan

CHAPTER 1:
MY UNCLE NATHAN

I publicly introduced my great-uncle Nathan to the world when I became the pastor of Martindale Baptist Church in Martindale, Texas. I shared the Uncle Nathan stories as modern-day parables to illustrate my sermons, always adding the disclaimer that there are many Uncle Nathan stories…some of them are even true.

After several Sundays of my entertaining the congregation with the spiritual antics of Uncle Nathan, one of our members asked if there really was an Uncle Nathan. I assured him there really was and placed a picture of Uncle Nathan on the church bulletin board so all could see that he was not a figment of my imagination but a real person.

Several weeks later, the same man came to see me with a smile on his face. He said, "There really was an Uncle Nathan." He went on to explain: "I was visiting with an elderly aunt in San Angelo, and I asked her if she had ever heard of a Rev. Nathan Bullock. She rolled her eyes and said, 'Lord, yes. He is the reason that your Uncle Willie is a Methodist.'" This was the only time the mention of Uncle Nathan brought such a response, and I'm not sure that I want to know the rest of the story.

Yes, Uncle Nathan was a very real person. A Baptist preacher, he was called a circuit rider because he served several churches in a geographical area. His mission field was in the Concho River country of West Texas. To me, he is a myth, a legend, and a very real, warm person whom I met only once when I about eight years old.

According to *the Record of Baptist Statistics* for 1895, N.D. Bullock was the pastor of the First Baptist Church of Sterling City, Texas. The following transcript of a newspaper article from the *Fort Worth Star-Telegram* gives a glimpse of the man:

> "The Rev. Bullock Pioneered in Saving Souls When Texas Was Raw Frontier…He Served Many Churches.
>
> A horse and buggy preacher with 47 years' service in West Texas, the Rev. Nathan Davis Bullock passed on to ride the circuit in heaven."
>
> "When he came to the district in 1894, he was the only ordained minister in nine counties. 'I was in great demand then,' recalls the Rev. Mr. Bullock, 'and people were good about going to church. I sometimes thought it was because they didn't have anywhere else to go.'"

During these years of riding around the countryside in a double buggy, preaching and baptizing in sparsely scattered communities all over West Texas, Uncle Nathan organized eight churches, baptized hundreds of people, and traveled thousands of miles over trails and plains where there were no paved roads until after 1915.

CHAPTER 2:
NO PLACE FOR PREACHING

Sometimes a preacher brought religion to places where very little pertaining to the spirit ever entered. Driving west on Interstate 10 between Ozona and El Paso, one will cross the Pecos River. Shortly after crossing the river, one will see a sign for Sheffield. Take that exit and experience a spectacular ride down into the Pecos River Valley to the small community of Sheffield.

The springs on the Pecos River that are popular even today were known to be a gathering place for nomadic Indians well back into the prehistoric age. The first in the area came with Spanish explorer Gaspar Castagno de Sosa and his men who traveled from Mexico north up the Pecos River.

In 1880 John Cannon purchased some land along the river for his ranch. It included the river crossing where he laid out a town site. In the succeeding years a saloon, schoolhouse, and general store brought settlers to the area. About 1900 John Sheffield, who owned the store, became the first postmaster and gave the town a name.

In these early years, cattlemen, sheepherders, travelers, and outlaws were drawn to the Pecos River crossing and the springs of the Pecos. Sheffield became known as Warfield in that era because of the reports of shootings and mayhem that were heard daily from the area. It was a place that could certainly use some hard preaching but was generally avoided by itinerant preachers. However, it probably won't surprise you...Uncle Nathan didn't just take on the challenge for Sheffield, but also delighted in the opportunity to preach to every town down the road!

When he arrived in Sheffield, he entered the saloon, placed his Bible on the bar, and announced that he would be holding services in the schoolhouse every night that week. It was his wish that all would come. That night he went to the schoolhouse and found it dark; there were no lights in the building. Electricity was still several years away. But undeterred, if anyone came, he was ready to preach. As he stood on the porch waiting, he saw a light coming from the saloon. The saloon owner brought the large coal oil

 lantern that hung over the bar in his saloon. He was followed by the patrons from the bar who were left without light. Nathan had a week of preaching and undoubtedly left Sheffield a better place.

Another time a man in Garden City pulled his six shooter and

threatened to kill Uncle Nathan because he had baptized his wife. "He was a wicked scoundrel," chuckled Uncle Nathan, "a transient scum of a feller, and he's got me as I was driving the buggy back home. Luckily, I had a big man with me that I was giving a ride when this fellow stepped up to the buckboard and said, 'Bullock, if you ever set foot in my house again, I'll kill you!'"

"It just tickled me to death," Uncle Nathan said. "He threatened to leave his wife and home because his wife had turned Baptist. But he went away and came back home in two days."

When Uncle Nathan was pastor at Sterling City, he learned of a little church in Mitchell County at a place called Schoolhouse, 60 miles away. "There are a few good people there," said Uncle Nathan. But with no pastor the congregation had almost decided to disband the church. Uncle Nathan heard the call and headed for Westbrook.

He had planned on two days for the trip with a stopover at a friendly ranch. But when darkness came, "It felt like a curtain." Uncle Nathan was in the middle of a prairie with no tracks indicating the direction of Westbrook. Somehow, he got off the road and soon found himself miles from anywhere.

"I hobbled the horses and crawled into the back of my buggy to sleep, supperless and without breakfast," said Uncle Nathan. "I'd been sleeping for a little while when the most awful howling you ever heard began. I peeked out and there was a gang of lobo wolves, as big as two-year-old steers, howling away, spooking the horses and prowling around the buggy. That was the longest night I ever spent."

When he woke up he found he had spent the night in the middle of the Conway Ranch in a 100–section ranch. He drove on to Westbrook where he held two services the next day. He traveled there every month for the next two years, saving the church.

In later years Uncle Nathan's nephew, Sam, raised his family on Conway Ranch where he was foreman and manager. One of his hands was his brother, John, who was a working cowboy until the mid-1930s. In his memoirs he told much about the trip to Scurry County, and he wrote about large cattle drives that he worked in 1915. I had not been aware of any large trail drives after 1900.

An interview with Mr. Conway in an Abilene newspaper told about the terrible drought of 1915. The drought led to the death of many of the cattle in the central Texas ranges. The ranchers got their herds together and drove them north to Canyon in the Texas panhandle where they could find water and forage.

CHAPTER 3:
BOARD OF EDUCATION

The children were educated in the traditional one-room schoolhouse where all grades studied together, usually under a hired "professor." Sometimes it was simply the oldest student who had finished all the grades.

Those were the days when the "board of education" was anything from a willow switch to a leather saddle tug. Nathan's brother, John C. Bullock, had all nine of his children in such a school.

John Hamilton was the youngest of the four older boys. He would

much rather be helping his pa than sitting in school and went to school as little as possible. When he was in school, he was the most likely to get a whipping.

So it was that one day the teacher, a hired professor, whipped him with a saddle tug far beyond the normal whipping; it drew blood in several places. Later, after school, the teacher had remorse for his work and fear for what John Sr would do. He went to the farm and got down on his knees to Pa and asked forgiveness. Pa had not seen the whelps and bruises, so he forgave the man. Ma, however, who had seen his work was waiting for him to come down to the house with an iron skillet behind her back. Fortunately for him, he went the other way. The next day the teacher was fired.

John Hamilton later had a wild west show and made his living breaking horses to saddle for the ranchers. He had a standing reward for any horse he couldn't ride.

CHAPTER 4:
THE CAMP MEETING

It is difficult for us in the 21st century to realize there was a time when the only thing people had to do for fun was to go to church. However, my children cannot remember when there was no television. My grandchildren don't remember when there was no computer, and my great grandchildren don't remember the birth of "Alexa."

In Uncle Nathan's day, about twice a year several pastors would unite and have a tent revival or sometimes a brush arbor meeting. For a tent revival a large tent would be set up for preaching the Word. For a brush arbor the pastors would go out in the country and cobble together a pulpit area out of trees and brush where the preaching would be done. Then word would be sent around the country that preaching was being held at such an hour every night (sometimes they went through the daytime hours as well) and invite all the ranchers,the cowboys and all their kin to come to the meeting. Regardless of the number of congregants there would be mighty preaching. Each night several pastors would take turns carrying the congregation to the foot of the cross. Sometimes these meetings would last for three or four weeks.

As you can tell from my narrative, these meetings lasted way into the night. At some time during the night the parents would put their babies to sleep in the wagons. Occasionally, teenage boys slipped out of the meeting and switched the babies around. When the meeting was over and everyone came out to go home, no one bothered to check what baby they had. After all, who wants to wake up a sleeping baby? You can imagine the confusion when they got home and discovered they did not have the right child.

My mother loved to tell stories of things that happened at these camp meetings. Her favorite story, one she told many times, was about a man responding to the altar call to accept Jesus as his savior. His wife, a large woman who had been praying for years for his salvation, jumped up, waving her arms, and exclaiming, "Thank you, Jesus. I am just so happy I could fly."

Mother's little sister, Ruth, snuggled close to their father. She pulled on his sleeve and said, "She can't, though, can she, Papa?"

Uncle Nathan recalls one of these meetings at Stiles in Reagan County. It was held in a 30' x 40' tent, attended by 150 people each day and lasted for 10 days straight. Ranchers from Sterling City, Ozona, and Garden City came with their families and slept on the ground.

Nathan rode 150 miles to that meeting. Two old ranch cooks barbecued beef that was donated by the ranchers and chickens were roasted for all. "My, I never saw people enjoy anything more," Uncle Nathan observed.

Uncle Nathan was also pastor at Crystal Ball for a year, Mortensen for two years, Sterling for two years, Atwater Valley for three years, Garden City for two years, Midway for twelve years, Hardin for a short time: Eola for two two-year periods, and Harriet for five. He was also pastor at Tennyson, Tankersley and "a lot of others I can't remember," Uncle Nathan said.

"Oh, I've done a whole lot of preaching, such as it was," he says, looking back on his 56 years as a minister, "and people seemed to think I was good."

Throughout my growing up years, family reunions were highly anticipated and important to the Bullock clan. It was from those gatherings that I gained words of wisdom and the understanding of life from many of the men of great integrity. They loved to laugh, especially at each other. Although they did not say so, I strongly suspect that many of their stories stretched the truth.

Many of these stories were shared as modern-day parables before my sermons when I was pastor of Martindale Baptist Church in Martindale, Texas, and Hill Country Church in San Marcos, Texas.

CHAPTER 5:
WEST TEXANS

West Texans are known for their slow manner of speech or drawl, it's called. One of our sons, Kevin, had a career as an air traffic controller with the FAA.

His first assignment was in the Concho River country at the airport in San Angelo. After he had been there for about a year, I asked him what was the hardest thing about his job.

His answer was, "West Texas pilots."

"What is it with West Texas pilots?" I asked.

He answered, "You have to visualize the situation. I'll have an airplane in my sector, and I will say to the pilot, 'Cessna 454, you

have military jet traffic at 3 o'clock. Report on sighting.' Nothing happens. Then after a while there will be a click on the radio and I will hear,' T o w e r, ...w o u l d ... y o u ...r e p e a t ...t h a t ...l a s t ...t r a n s m i s s i o n?' I just want to say, 'Buddy, if you haven't seen it now, you're not going to.'"

Unfortunately, being born just a few miles east of the headwaters of the Brazos River, I share that West Texas affliction. I strongly suspect that Uncle Nathan did also. It's for that reason that I kept my sermons short because, for us born west of the Trinity River, a short sermon can take quite a while. When we really get wound up, we can make the congregation late getting to the cafeteria for lunch. Sometimes we can do that with the opening prayer alone.

One week Uncle Nathan told the congregation he would be preaching on the sin of lying the next Sunday and urged them to read Mark, chapter 17. The next Sunday he asked everyone who had read chapter 17 in the Gospel of Mark to raise their hand.

Almost everyone raised their hand only to learn there is no chapter 17 in that Gospel. That was their lesson on lying.

When the Bullocks first came to Texas, Indian raids still occurred. One time when Uncle Nathan was a child and was out in the garden he looked up and saw a band of Indians coming over the hill. He dropped the hoe, ran for the house, and jumped underneath the table for safety.

He was there when he watched his father walk out of the house with the axe to chop some wood, without a word of warning from his son.

In less than a minute his daddy was back in the house, barring the door and grabbing for his gun on the wall. For the next 10 minutes they watched the men passing by their house. They turned out to be friendly, but sure scared the family. After it was all over, Nathan told his dad that he'd seen those Indians coming.

"For goodness' sake, son," his daddy said, "why didn't you tell me?"

"Well," Nathan said, "I figured you had seen how scared I was, and you would've asked.".

CHAPTER 6:
WEST TEXAS WEATHER

KFYO, the voice of the South Plains summed it up with: Weather it's cold or weather it's hot, we will have weather, weather it all or not.

Texas Barometer

Tail still and dry—Fair weather

Tail swinging back and forth— Windy

Tail swinging— A storm

Tail frozen——Cold really cold.

Flash flood waters down the Concho River could be disastrous.

But even the occasional rainstorms did not keep Uncle Nathan from making his rounds. On one occasion when the rains had been extremely heavy for several days, he was forced to seek shelter with a rancher and his family. After the fourth consecutive day of steady rain the rancher asked Uncle Nathan, "Is it ever going to stop?"

Uncle Nathan responded, biblically, "Well, BrotherWilliams, since the rainbow it always has."

Mrs. Williams, not satisfied with that answer, said,"Well, Brother, looks like you could speak to the Lord and let him know we've had enough."

With a mischievous look on his face, Uncle Nathan responded with, "I'll do what I can, but you've got to remember I'm in sales and He is in management."

Aunt Maggie was afraid of storms. They had been through a tornado and a flood so when it started to thunder it was time to head for the storm cellar. It was particularly bad when the storm came at night and the thunder would shake the roof. Nothing would do but that Uncle Nathan go take a look at the weather.

Uncle Nathan felt his way into the living room and into the kitchen to the back door. At least he thought it was the back door; it was a lot of trouble to light up the oil lamp. In the dark he opened the door to the icebox. He peered in and then he exclaimed, "Maggie! Maggie, get up! Lord help us. It's darker than Egypt outside and the whole world smells like collard greens."

It'd been a terrible drought. Several months passed with no rain so Uncle Nathan called a special prayer meeting to ask God to give them some needed fresh water. Brother Wiggins, a rancher who had already lost several head of cattle, stood up and prayed, "Dear God, we sure do need water. We would love it if you'd send us some rain. I know that praying ain't gonna help until the wind is out of the west."

No place in the world can get colder faster than on the West Texas plains. They call them blue northers because they come in so fast from the north. You had to be flexible living in that country.

It was on such a day that Brian was working his fence line in his model T pickup truck. He had seen the dark blue sky in the north; he knew what was coming. But he stayed with the job just a little too long. He tried to start his truck. He would crank it; it would turn over; he would jump in and the motor would die. He looked up toward heaven and he said, "God help me get this truck started.

Bless his heart; he froze out on the prairie that night. The archangel could see the fellow was a little miffed about something and said, "Why, Brian,you don't seem to be really glad to be here."

"Well, you didn't get my old truck started or I wouldn't be here. I prayed, and I prayed, but I guess y'all didn't hear me."

The angel slapped his knees and laughed out loud. "Was that you? We hadn't heard from you in a long time, so no one recognized your voice. We started a pickup truck for a farmer up in Idaho.

CHAPTER 7:
EHARMONY.COM, 1890

During the settling of this part of Texas, it was mainly men who came. They came to start homesteads, farms and ranches and to begin new lives where resources were plentiful, spaces were wide and open, and there was a lot more freedom than back east. However, the many single men who went west soon found

themselves to be lonely.

They may or may not have had male friends nearby. Either way, it was no substitute for having female companionship. There were too few single women for the number of single men in the west.

The men could not travel away from their land and risk it being claimed or taken over by someone else while they were gone. So, they advertised in eastern newspapers for wives.

These women needed to find husbands elsewhere, in places far away from where they lived. Surprisingly, there was no shortage of women who answered these mail order bride ads. Many frontier marriages were made this way. Deacon Willis and his wife had been married for 50 years.

Theirs had been a fruitful and happy marriage. Uncle Nathan went by to give them his best wishes and congratulations.

"Brother Willis, you have had a good marriage. You certainly found a good woman."

"She is that, Brother Bullock. It is all I can do sometimes to keep from telling her I love her."

In those days folks pretty much stuck it out no matter how tough it got, and the couple hung on through stormy times.

Down the road, Herman Taner and his wife were also celebrating their 50th wedding anniversary. So Uncle Nathan went out to wish them a happy anniversary, only to find Brother Taner sitting dejectedly on the front porch of the ranch house. "What's the matter, Brother?" Uncle Nathan asked.

"I woke up this morning," he said. "I looked up and my wife was standing beside the bed. I smiled and said, 'Good morning, honey bunch. Happy anniversary." She looked at me and said, "Don't you honey bunch me. This has been the most miserable 50 years of my life. I wish I had never married you; I wish I'd never met you." After a pause, she continued, "And I think it's only fair to tell you that I am praying to the Lord that he takes one of us home." A longer pause. "And when he does, I'm going to live with my sister.".

CHAPTER 8:
GONE TO TEXAS

People were moving west and claiming the land for farming and ranching. Every day Uncle Nathan made his rounds to find new families

.One morning he came upon a new family just completing their dugout, literally a hole in the ground with a roof on it, that would become their temporary home. A little girl, seven or eight years old, was playing in the yard.

"Good morning, honey. How long have you folks been in Texas?" he asked

"We came last month," she said.

"Have you found a church yet?" he asked.

The young lady looked down at the ground and sort of twisted her foot back and forth before she answered, "No, sir, my mom said

God hasn't got toTexas yet…And she's not sure he's coming."

On another occasion, he came upon a newly built home where a lad of 12 or so was weeding the garden.

'Good morning, young fella. Is your mama home?" Uncle Nathan asked.

The boy answered, "You don't think I would be here in this garden if she was gone, do you?"

A widow with five children moved into the community. Uncle Nathan asked some of his churchwomen to visit her and see if there was anything they could do to help her. After the visit, they reported back to the pastor that she had very little and especially the children needed new clothes. They took Widow Brown shopping and bought new clothes for her and for all the children. Sunday came and they expected to see Widow Brown and her children at church. There was no sign of them, so they said to themselves, one of the children must be sick. The next week they were watching on the porch of the church and still no Widow Brown.

On Monday morning the church ladies were on theirway to visit Miz Brown and see why she had not been to church. They knocked on the door. Not wanting to appear too forward, the ladies simply said, "Mrs. Brown, we missed you all at church the last two Sundays."

"Oh, yes'um, we were in church both Sundays," she said, while the ladies looked at each other. "When the kids and I got all dressed up, we went to the Piscopalian church with the fine folk."

CHAPTER 9:
THE RANCH HANDS

One of the things that Uncle Nathan enjoyed the most was visiting with the ranch hands around the campfire and chuck wagon at the end of the day's work to share the gospel.

One night he asked if anyone knew the Lord's Prayer.

A gnarled old ranch hand, Charles, raised his hand. "I do, I do," he said.

Buck was standing over by the chuck wagon. He had been listening to the conversation and he didn't believe that Charles knew the Lord's Prayer. "Now, Charles," he said, "you know you don't know the Lord's Prayer. Bet you five dollars."

With that Charles stood up, took off his old Stetson, bowed his head and said, "Now I lay me down to sleep, I pray the Lord my soul to keep. If I should die before I wake, I pray the Lord my soul to take."

"Well, bless my soul," said Buck. "I sure didn't think you could do it! Here's the five dollars."

Later Buck said to Charles, "You were talking so low I could hardly hear a thing you said."

To which Charles replied, "Well, Buck, I wasn't speaking to you."

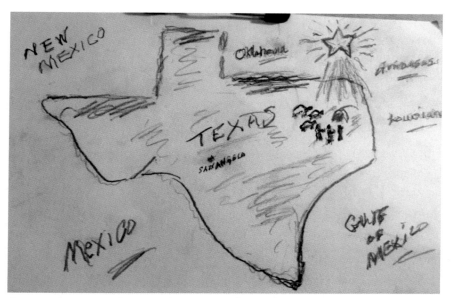

On another occasion, as they went through the Bible study, Uncle Nathan asked, "Who can tell me where Jesus was born?" Buck raised his hand first this time and said, "I think it was Kilgore (town in East Texas)."

"No, Buck, it wasn't in Kilgore."

Then Charles spoke up and said, "I believe it must've been at Lufkin (another town in East Texas") No, fellows," Uncle Nathan said, "it wasn't any of those. Jesus was born in Palestine."

Buck said, "Well, dang it. I knew it was in East Texas some place."

Around the campfire Uncle Nathan was teaching on the destruction of Sodom and Gomorrah. He explained that Lot was told to take his wife and flee out of the city and not look back, but his wife looked back and was turned into a pillar of salt. He asked if there were any questions. After a while little Billy raised his hand and asked,"Pastor, what happened to the flea?"

In his Bible lesson one night he told about Jonah and the fish that took him to Nineveh. Lester, the agnostic, said, "You don't really believe there was a fish that big, do you?"

Tex came back with the obvious response, "God can do anything He wants to."

Uncle Nathan closed the discussion with, "When we get to heaven, we can ask Jonah."

"Yeah," said Lester. "What if Jonah isn't there?"

"Then," Uncle Nathan replied, "I guess you can ask him."

When Uncle Nathan went into a new community, he often had to preach at the schoolhouse for lack of a church building. On one occasion he announced services at 7:00 that evening at the local schoolhouse.

Seven o'clock came and no one showed up. Then, about 7:15 one lone cowboy came in and sat down right up front. Uncle Nathan said he reckoned they would wait a few minutes and see if anyone else came. After another twenty minutes he suggested maybe waiting until the next night.

"Well," the cowboy said, "parson, if we go out to feed the cows and only one old cow shows up we don't let it go hungry."

Encouraged by that, Uncle Nathan opened his Bible and began to preach the Word. The cowboy was attentive, so he preached halfway through the New Testament before he gave out.

The cowboy said, "You know, parson, that was a powerful message but out here if we go out to feed the cows and only one cow shows up, we don't drop the whole load."

One night he was asked what is the best position for prayer. One said, "I think you have to get on your knees, close your eyes and hold your hands together under your chin." Old John said, "You don't have to do all that, you just bow your head, close your eyes and pray."

Tex had been listening to these comments and he said, "Well, I don't know about you guys but the best praying I ever did was on the back of that killer horse I rode at the Fat Stock Show in Ft Worth last year."

Later Uncle Nathan was explaining about King Ahab and Queen Jezebel. "Kings and queens were all-powerful in those days," he said. "But we know a higher power, don't we?"

He waited for a reply. Finally, Luke spoke up, "I'm not sure this is what you are looking for but aces will do it."

Uncle Nathan was trying to teach the cowboys the concept of heaven or what you must do to be saved. "If you entered the Fort Worth Fat Stock Show Rodeo and rode the meanest horse in the remuda for 10 minutes, would that get you into heaven?"

"Well," Lester said, "only if'n you was throwed and kilt."

One evening after the Bible study Uncle Nathan asked Deacon Jones, the owner of the ranch, "Bob,how's that new hand working out for you?"

"Well, pastor," the deacon said, "I reckon if he paid me for what he breaks we should be near even.".

CHAPTER 10:
FUNNY THINGS HAPPEN AT CHURCH

Calvinists prohibited laughter in church services. They thought to be worshipful one had to be long-faced and serious. That all goes along with the idea that God is a serious God, one who has a long face and seeks only to punish wrongdoers.

Jesus taught us to be joyful, smile and to love God. As children we sing, "Jesus loves me, this I know, for the Bible tells me so."

Someone has said, "If you want to make God laugh, just tell him your plans." Another said, "If you think God does not have a sense of humor, just look in the mirror."

The truth is that some of the funniest things happen in church. Funny things happen during church services, funny things happen in the choir, funny things happen in the bulletin, funny things happen at weddings and even at funerals. If you go to church and have not had a good laugh yet, just hold onto the back of the pew—sooner or later you will see something funny.

Baptists have two big "no's:" no drinking and no dancing. Both were often the theme of Uncle Nathan's sermons. One Sunday he held forth on the subject of liquor. It was a strong dose of don'ts. Don't drink beer; I would take all the beer and pour it in the Concho River. Don't drink whiskey; I would take all the whiskey and pour it into the Concho. Don't drink gin; I would take all the gin and pour it in the Concho. Don't drink demon rum; I would take all the rum and pour it in the Concho.

Over at the organ sister Smith was getting nervous. She had planned the next hymn to be 'Shall We Gather at the River?'

It is a good thing that Uncle Nathan lived and served before many of the modern technical wonders became a part of our lives. One pastor recounted that during one of his sermons an elderly lady suddenly took her lap robe and threw it over her head and began talking on her cell phone. For all to hear, she said, "Hello? Hello? No! No! No, he is not done yet! I told you he was long-winded!

Hold on, I am in the auditorium, let me move to the lobby."

Not everyone prays out loud so it's important for the pastor to know who to call on for prayer and who not to. One night he had a visiting pastor who called upon Deacon Jones to "lead us to the throne of grace with a word of prayer."

Deacon Jones was one of those who does not pray in public. Pulling all his courage together, Deacon Jones stood up, gripped the back of the pew in front of him, bowed his head and told us to bow our heads and close our eyes in prayer... and then he left.

At one of the many churches that Uncle Nathan pastored he apparently said the wrong thing as far as one of the members was concerned. As he left the church, he told him, "It's just a good thing we like your wife." It is true that sometimes that's the only reason churches keep their pastor around.

By the beginning of the 20th century, it was already being talked about that there was a need for a new English translation of the holy Scriptures. In a church council meeting one of the deacons involved in the discussion of whether there was a need for a new translation said, "Well, I can tell you this, if the King James Version was good enough for Paul and Silas, it is good enough for me."

At the wedding of one of Uncle Nathan's favorite young couples he had intended to add a special touch by reading 1 John 4:18: "There is no fear in love; instead, perfect love drives out fear." He had marked it with a paperclip on the top of the pertinent page. Unfortunately, he opened his Bible to John 4:18 and read it at the wedding: "For you have had five husbands, and the man you now have is not your husband."

.

CHAPTER 11:
HUMOR AT FUNERALS/CEMETERIES

Grady Nutt, the well-known pastor and humorist of the 1970s, said that while funny things happen at funerals, you couldn't really talk about them until later and then in private conversation. He said that if the pastor got up in the pulpit on Sunday and started his message with, "A funny thing happened at Sister Simpson's funeral Thursday… he would be run out of town." " And," Grady said, "he ought to be."

Sister Shipley had been a member of the congregation for many years and was known for her sharp tongue and love for gossip. It might be rightly said that very few attending the funeral were feeling a great deal of sorrow at her loss.

As Uncle Nathan was finishing his funeral remarks at the cemetery there was a streak of lightning and the Earth was shaken by a mighty roll of thunder punctuated his remarks.

Uncle Nathan looked up and silently thought to himself, "Well, Lord, I see she made it."

Old Brother Alden was married to the shrew of the county for 30 years, when Mrs. Alden took sick and passed away. Uncle Nathan officiated at the funeral in the home and several of the ranch hands served as pallbearers. As they carried the coffin out of the house and down the walk, Jake stumbled against the gate post and dropped the coffin. The lid popped open, and Sister Alden sat up, totally revived from a profound coma. She lived several more years, making life generally miserable around the ranch

Finally. Uncle Nathan was called upon once again to preach her funeral; she had succumbed to influenza. As the pallbearers maneuvered the coffin down the walk, Brother Alden was heard to caution, "Brother, work her through right easy like."

On another occasion when the deceased was a rascal and a renegade and widely suspected of being a horse thief, Uncle Nathan set his eulogy to the deeds. "I would love to say something good about the late departed but anything I could say has already

been said about skeeters, chiggers and warts."

One of the members of his congregation asked Uncle Nathan what he wanted said about him when he was "called to the Lord." He replied that he wanted a simple poem placed on his tombstone:

The people need not shed their tears:

Though he was dead,

he was not more dead

than they had been for years.

Nasty Bill was another "hellion" who passed away with very little mourning. Uncle Nathan was called upon to do the "plant'n and read'n" over him.

Nathan stood at the pulpit, looked out at the handfulof folks who had gathered and said, "Folks, we may not miss old Bill much and will not likely meet him in the hereafter, but we have just got to remember that there was times when he was not as bad as he was at other times."

Sometimes Uncle Nathan would be truly at a loss for words, such as at Oscar Cartwright's passing away. Oscar had never breathed a straight breath or walked a straight mile or stay sober more than 20 minutes in his whole sordid life. Nobody would miss him when he went to his eternal reward.

"Preacher, what are you going to say at Oscar's funeral?" he was asked "There's not much you can say," he answered."You know,

Oscar can't get into heaven. Why, he couldn't make it with a double eagle gold piece and a written recommendation signed by three of the original apostles."

Many times, pastors are called upon to conduct funerals for people that they hardly know. This can lead to some embarrassing moments. of the service. Once the pastor who had responsibility for the service did not show up and so the funeral directorat the last minute called upon Uncle Nathan, "Nathan, can you take over?" And he did.

He began the service: "I did not know Mr. Nash well, but I have been told of his outstanding character and his love for the Lord. He was preceded in death by his beloved wife, Irma, and so this morning they are standing hand-in-hand in the great beyond."

At this point a white-haired gentleman in the first row stood up and raised his hand. "Pastor," he said, "I'm Jim Jacobs. This here funeral is for my wife, Irma, who lays here in this coffin before you."

At the funeral home, the pastor often did not see the family prior to the service. This was especially true if he did not know the family well.

What normally happened was the pastor arrived at the funeral home and was escorted back into a quiet placewhere he could contemplate what he would say. Then when it was time for the funeral the funeral director would escort him to a back door into the sanctuary. He would go in and be seated; the curtain would remain drawn until time for the eulogy. And so, it was with some consternation when the curtain was opened and Uncle Nathan stood up to speak, he realized that he did not know anyone in the congregation, family, or visitors. He was at the wrong funeral home.

Emma and Miss Betty Pat were old maid sisters and they lived together all their lives. When their older sister, Rose, passed away, Nathan was called to officiate at the funeral. It was a solemn occasion. Nevertheless, it was a celebration of Sister Rose's life. Emma and Betty Pat sat on the front pew right beside the casket.

When the funeral was over and the pallbearers had removed the casket, the pastor noted that Miss Emma and Miss Betty Pat were still sitting in the pew. Emma was quietly holding Ms. Betty's hand; They seemed to be in an attitude of prayer. Uncle Nathan went over and touched Miss Emma on the shoulder and said, "Miss Emma, the funeral is over."

Ms. Emma opened her eyes and said, "Yes, I know but it was such a beautiful service and it's so quiet here, I decided I'd stay here a minute. And besides, I think Miss Betty died and I didn't want to interrupt the service."

Then Uncle Nathan was asked to perform a burial of an indigent man with no family or friends. Not knowing where the cemetery was, when he eventually arrived an hour late, the hearse was nowhere in sight. The backhoe was next to the open hole, and the workmen were sitting under a tree eating lunch. He walked up to the open grave and found the vault lid already in place. Feeling guilty because of his tardiness, he preached a committal message, sending the deceased to the great beyond in style.

As he returned to his buggy, he overheard one of the workmen say to the other, "I've been putting in septic tanks for twenty years and

I ain't never seen anything like that."

Uncle Nathan had a high regard for the sanctity of marriage, but there were times when all the traditional parts of a marriage ceremony were impossible. And so it was when he came upon a young couple building a house on their farm. As he did with most everyone, he asked if there was anything, he could do for them

"Well, parson, "said the man, "there is one thing. We been so busy since we come to Texas, we haven't had time to get rightly married. Wonder if you can take care that while you're here?"

"Well, okay," said Uncle Nathan. "Don't guess you have a license. We've got no witnesses, but I reckon it's the right thing that you

want to do." About that time a scraggly old farm dog came walking up, wagging its tail, "Well", said Uncle Nathan, "I believe we've got ourselves a witness."

And so it was that the young couple became husband and wife there on the prairie with only an old farm dog as a witness. But they had done the right thing.

At the wedding of one of Uncle Nathan's favorite couples he had intended to add a special touch by reading 1 John 4:18: "There is no fear in love; instead, perfect love drives out fear." He had marked it with a paperclip on the top of the pertinentpage. Unfortunately, he opened his Bible to John 4:18 and read it at the wedding: "For you have had five husbands, and the man you now have is not your husband."

By the beginning of the 20th century, it was already being talked about that there was a need for a new English translation of the holy Scriptures. In a church council meeting one of the deacons involved in the discussion of whether there was a need for a new translation said, "Well, I can tell you this, if the King James Version was good enough for Paul and Silas, it is good enough for me."

Out on the range you raised a lot of your own help. Large families of 10 or 12 children were very common in the early days of Texas. Still, the birth of a new child was worth a pastoral call. Deacon Ellis had a new son and, true to his calling, Uncle Nathan went for a visit. "Well, Brother Ellis," asked Uncle Nathan, "what did you name your new son?"

"Brother Bullock," said the deacon, "you know we've named all our kids out of the Bible. There was Matthew, Mark, Luke, John,

Paul, and Andrew but we had a hard time finding another one. So we just looked through the Book and decided that we would name him Psalumsciv ."

Uncle Nathan had to think about that for a while. "Psalumsciv … Psalumsciv … I don't believe I remember that in the good book," he told Deacon Ellis.

"Oh, yes, sir," said the deacon, "I'll show it to you." And so, he brought out the old family Bible and sure enough there was it was, Psalm CIV… Psalm 104.

Frontier pastors did not get paid much in those days (most pastors still don't), but they had a good humor about it. When asked what he charged to perform a wedding, Uncle Nathan would always say, "Well, you can just pay me whatever you think she's worth."

Divorce was rare in those days. Not all marriages were happy, but people generally just lived with it, believing in the promise at the wedding ceremony, "until death do us part." People didn't often come to Uncle Sam for counseling but here one morning sat the Wilsons. They had been married for 35 years but they were contemplating divorce.

After listening to them for a while it was apparent that neither really wanted a divorce, they were still in love and to break it up seemed ludicrous. The conversation went like this:

Nathan: "You know, after listening to you I don't believe you have any grounds."

Sister: "Why, Brother Bullock, you know we have 40 acres just in cotton."

Nathan: "I mean it doesn't seem like you all have a grudge."

Brother: "No, we don't have no grudge, just a carport."

Nathan: "No, no, I mean it just doesn't seem to me that there's any reason for you to get a divorce."

Together: "Well, I guess you're right, but we just can't seem to communicate."

After 60 years of marriage there come times when a man has that special sense of being in love. After supper one night, Nathan got down on a knee and said "Darlin', I have two questions I need to ask you: Do you love me as much as you did the day we got married?"

"Of course, I do, you old goof. You know I do," she said. "What's your other question?"

"Well, I was just kind of wondering, maybe you would help me up."

One Sunday after the sermon a little girl came up to him with a book in her hand and asked, "Pastor, have you read the book, *101Things to Do During a Boring Sermon?*"

Nathan and his wife were coming to the Clarks for lunch after church. Little Ed asked, "Is he the one that advertises?"

Everyone gave him a puzzled look and dad asked, "What do you mean, advertises?"

Ed said, "You know, the one who advertises people in the water?"

It was Palm Sunday and Deacon McKay's boy, Tony, had to stay home because he had a sore throat. When the family returned home, they were carrying palm fronds that had been used in the worship service. His father explained that the people waved palm branches when Jesus rode Into town.

"People on the road as Jesus came over them on his donkey," his father told him.

"Wouldn't you know it," Tony moaned, "the one Sunday I don't go to Sunday School and he comes."

The Sunday School lesson had been all about Satan, the evil one. Two lads on their way homefrom church were in deep concentration and conversation on the subject.

"Darned if I know," replied Josh. "I've been thinking about it and I would not be surprised if it turns out like Santa Claus, just your pa dressed in a red suit..

CHAPTER 12:
BUSINESS MEETINGS

In the old days, many of the churches, if they had property of their own, would have a burying ground close to the church. These often led to busy discussions at the church meetings.

Like the time that Deacon Hawkins made a motion to put a fence around the burying ground. Aaron McKinsey, one of those that only came to business meetings occasionally, spoke against the motion, stating that it wasn't necessary "because them that's in can't get out and them that's out don't want in."

Business meetings are one of Satan's favorite tools to destroy the church. Here are some of the things that churches have split over: (I am sure that Uncle Nathan would have had a long list of his own.)

- appropriate length of the worship leader's beard.

- if a clock in the worship center should be removed.

- type of filing cabinet to purchase; black or brown and two, three are four drawers.

- which pictures of Jesus to put up in the foyer.

- discovery the church budget was $0.10 off; someone finally gave a dime to settle the issue.

- purchase a weed eater or not. It took two business meetings to resolve.

- deviled eggs allowed at church meals or not.

- who has the authority to buy postage stamps for the church.

- using the term "potluck" instead of "pot blessing."

- who has access to the copy machine.

- have gluten-free communion bread or not.

- should the church allow people to wear black T-shirts, since black is the color of the devil.

- An argument about whether the fake, dusty, plants should be removed from the podium.

CHAPTER 13:
MORE BUSINESS

Uncle Nathan: A motion was made to put a lock on the outhouse. A simple yes or no motion, right?

Brother Bill: Point of order discussion on the floor that we put a lock on the outhouse. Discussion?

Uncle Nathan "The motion has had sufficient discussion; do I hear a call for a vote?"

Brother Bill: Pastor, there is still discussion on the insurance issue, I move the motion be tabled until the next business meeting.

Motion to table carries.

There were essentially two issues in the discussion:

1 The open outhouse implies a possible tort litigation. In other words, if somebody gets in there, we might have to pay.

2. Nobody is going to get in the outhouse. Nobody goes there so

we don't need a lock on it It's been there for 40 years without a lock and nobody got hurt or stole anything.

During the ensuing week a person or persons deposited the body of a dead horse in the outhouse. By Sunday nobody wanted to go there.

After the cleanup, without further discussion a shiny new lock was hanging on the outhouse door.

Uncle Nathan had noted that business meetings were often better attended than the Sunday morning services. That was because folks who don't come to anything else will make it to the business meeting, so they can vote against anything that costs money.

My favorite is the motion that was made to buy a new chandelier. After an hour's discussion, Farmer Jones arose once more and said, "I'm against it. First of all, nobody can play it, and second of all nobody can spell it. Besides, what we really need is lights."

Such misunderstandings were not uncommon among the unlettered folk of the West Texas frontier. Unfortunately, they happen all too often in the modern church, leading to divisiveness and hard feelings.

Short sermon: William Barclay the great Scottish linguist and theologian said that if two people believing themselves to be Christians who have anger or unforgiveness toward each other need to examine their salvation because the Holy Spirit dwelling in the Christian heart cannot quarrel against himself.

On one occasion, the business meeting had reached its climax. Uncle Nathan had urged the congregation to "pull together and no longer be satisfied with the status quo."

Aaron again rose to address the issue. "I agree with the pastor," he said "all except about that status quo. What we really need is to work together to get out of this mess that we are in."

In a community the pastors of the churches of all denominations would meet once or twice a year and discuss the evangelization of the area. Sometimes they would have lively discussions about the Bible and those things spiritual. So it was that while they were all very good friends, the rivalries ran deep.

After one especially good lunch while in a good mood, a Methodist minister asked Uncle Nathan why he followed the Baptist persuasion. "Well," Nathan answered candidly, "my daddy was a

Baptist, my granddaddy was a Baptist, so I guess it was natural that I would be one, too."

"So," said the Methodist minister, "I guess if your daddy and your granddaddy had been horse thieves, that would make you one, too."

"No," said Uncle Nathan, "if my daddy had been a horse thief and my granddaddy had been a horse thief, I strongly suspect I would've been a Methodist."

In one meeting Uncle Nathan and old Brother Wilcox from Eden were engaged in a friendly dispute. "It seems," said Brother Wilcox, "that we are engaged in a battle of wits between thee and me."

"No," Uncle Nathan answered, "I never fight with an unarmed man."

It is a matter of fact in Texas history that Stephen Austin once proclaimed he would rather have five horse thieves take up residence in his colony than one Baptist preacher. His reasoning was simple, he could hang the horse thief.

CHAPTER 14:
THE PROVERBS ACCORDING TO UNCLE NATHAN

- The Bible says that a feller and his wife should not ever go to bed mad. I guess they might as   well stay up and fight it out.

- Any jackass can kick down the barn door, but it takes a pretty good carpenter to build one.

- It's easier not to start something that it is to stop it after it gets going.

- It always seems to me that a fellow who works real hard gets mighty lucky.

- Fleas are not all bad. At least they give a dog something to think about.

- When you get yourself between a rock and a hard place, it seems to me that you got two choices: you can give up or you can climb out.

- Anybody can give advice to their kids as long as they're young enough to think you know what you're talking about.

- If you aren't sure how deep the water is, you best not step in with both feet.

- They say that nothing is for certain, but I am certain that nothing is uncertain.

- Some people skip church because it's too hot. It seems these folks haven't given hell much thought.

- The apostle Paul learned to be content in whatever state he was in. Near as I can figure he never got to Texas.

- Life is a lot like riding bicycle. If you just sit there, you're likely to fall off.

- I guess a fellow did not learn much the first time if he lets a mule kick him twice.

- Experience mainly helps you recognize a mistake when you do it.

West Texas was settled by people from all corners of the growing United States. However, they were largely English, Scots, Irish and Scots Irish from the south. They began to move west from the time English boots landed on the Atlantic shores. Three hundred years before the first Englishman walked our sacred soil the Spaniards had begun to explore and even to settle the land for their King or Queen and Country. Before them all these prairies, rivers and mountains were the province of numerous tribes of Native

Americans. The banks of the Concho River are said to have been home for the tribes at least as far back as 10,000 years.

As late as 1889 the land west of the present Interstate Highway 35 and north of the Rio Grande was known as Comancheria. There is one other legend of the Concho River country that needs to be told.

CHAPTER 15:
THE LADY IN BLUE

Uncle Nathan was not the first missionary to visit the Concho River Valley. Long before he traveled the prairies the Spanish padres brought Christianity and were surprised to find that Jesus had beaten them there.

The first of the Franciscans found native Americans wearing crosses and asking, "Are you the ones the Blue Lady said would come and baptize us?" Not only baptism but they also requested specific Christian instruction they had no way of knowing existed. They claimed that a beautiful woman had come and lived in their villages, teaching them about Jesus.

Strangely enough the story was known in Europe as well. In the small town of Agreda, Spain, a 22-year-old Franciscan nun, Maria, was writing books about her experiences. She wrote in vivid detail about her visits with the native people in the part of the New World that had been claimed by the king and queen for Spain.

To King Phillip of Spain, she became a spiritual guide and

confidant. It was impossible for her to be able to travel to these far-off lands. Soon, however, another blessed lady took her by the hand and transported her bi-locationally to the hills and prairies of the American Southwest.

Pictographs in stone in Arizona have left clear messages of her presence. The Spanish Inquisition was the protector of Catholic orthodoxy for almost four centuries of the Middle Ages in Europe. Holding themselves to be guardians of truth, they raised a question about the authenticity of Maria's visions. If they were simply the ravings of an overly imaginative girl, it should be stopped immediately.

The arm of the inquisition was long, indeed, and when Father Bienevedies returned from his work in New Mexico he was called before this tribunal and asked if there had been any indication found during his time in the field. During his time back in Spain Father Benevedies not only read her work but spent time with Sister Maria and reported that sign if the bilocation were indeed found throughout large southwestern regions of the north.

Here is an extract of her writings: From the year 1622 to 1625 at least 500 times she became present, as evangelizer, she says. Of these events she left a story: "*Look like To Me that one day, after having received our Lord, His Majesty showed me the whole world, and I knew the variety of bred things; how admirable is the Lord in the university of the land; He showed me with great clarity the multitude of creatures and souls that existed, and among them how few ones who were practicing the pure of the faith, and that were entering across the door of the baptism to be children of the holy Church. The heart was dividing of seeing that the copious redemption was not falling down but on so few ones. I knew the Gospel Compliment, which they are so many who are called but so few the select ones...*"

Between that much variety of those who were not practicing and confessing the faith, He declared me that the part of creatures that had better disposition to convert, and that his mercy was inclining more, were those of the New Mexico and other remote kingdoms of towards that part. The fact that The Most High demonstrated me his will in this, moved my spirit with new affections of love of God and of the neighbor, and to cry out of the profound of my soul for those souls." It was the missionary ardor of Sister Maria de Jesus, who only wanted to save souls for his dear Lord and that they all were praising the The Most High…

The story passes into the must of Folklore. America today is too wise and so filled with its demand for truth that can be measured will pass this off as just another fairy story.

Before you turn away, however I would remind you of the words of the Apostle Paul in the 1st chapter of Romans: Romans 1:15 – 22:

[15]So, as much as in me is, I am ready to preach the gospel to you that are at Rome also.

[16]For I am not ashamed of the gospel of Christ: for it is the power of God unto salvation to every one that believeth; to the Jew first, and also to the Greek.

[17]For therein is the righteousness of God revealed from faith to faith: as it is written, The just shall live by faith.

[18]For the wrath of God is revealed from heaven against all ungodliness and unrighteousness of men, who hold the truth in unrighteousness;

[19]Because that which may be known of God is manifest in them; for God hath shewed it unto them.

[20]For the invisible things of him from the creation of the world are clearly seen, being understood by the things that are made, even his eternal power and Godhead; so that they are without excuse:

[21]Because that, when they knew God, they glorified him not as God, neither were thankful; but became vain in their imaginations, and their foolish heart was darkened.

[22]Professing themselves to be wise, they became fools…

Disclaimer: Except for the Bullocks the names or personalities were not written to characterize any individual and any resemblance to any person, living or dead, is purely coincidental

ABOUT THE AUTHOR

Jerry M. Bullock is an ordained Baptist minister, father of seven children and grandfather to 25+ grandchildren and greatgrandchildren, and a retired Air Force colonel. He enjoys writing and hosts the Texas Country Church online: https://texascountrychurch.com/

Made in the USA
Coppell, TX
16 November 2021

65883561R00048